THE MYTHOLOGY LIBRARY

Egyptian Myths

Don Nardo

ReferencePoint Press

San Diego, CA

Printed in the United States

For more information, contact:
ReferencePoint Press, Inc.
PO Box 27779
San Diego, CA 92198
www.ReferencePointPress.com

LIBRARY OF CONGRESS CATALOGING-IN-PUBLICATION DATA

Names: Nardo, Don, 1947- author
Title: Egyptian myths / by Don Nardo.
Description: San Diego : ReferencePoint Press, 2026. | Series: The mythology library | Includes bibliographical references and index.
Identifiers: LCCN 2025024525 (print) | LCCN 2025024526 (ebook) | ISBN 9781678212322 library binding | ISBN 9781678212339 ebook
Subjects: LCSH: Mythology, Egyptian--Juvenile literature
Classification: LCC BL2441.3 .N3643 2026 (print) | LCC BL2441.3 (ebook)
LC record available at https://lccn.loc.gov/2025024525
LC ebook record available at https://lccn.loc.gov/2025024526

CONTENTS

GODS OF CREATION

Atum

Tefnut

Atum
(The First God)

Shu (God of Air) + **Tefnut** (Goddess of Moisture)

Geb (Earth God) + **Nut** (Sky Goddess)

Isis (Mother Goddess) + **Osiris** (Ruler of the Underworld)

Nephthys (God of Mummies) + **Seth** (God of War + Storms)

Horus (God of Kingship + Egypt's Protector)

Anubis (God of the Dead)

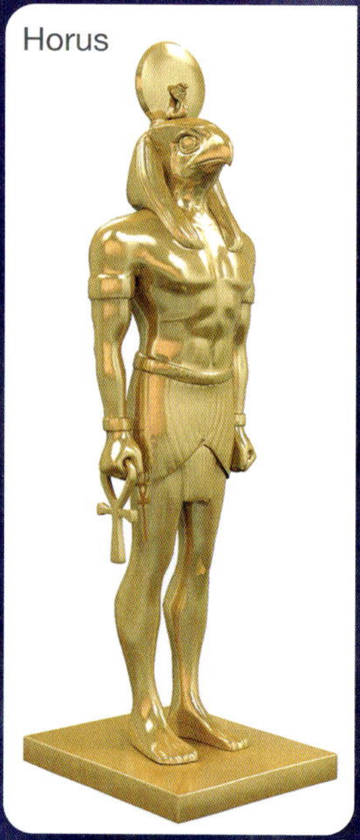
Horus

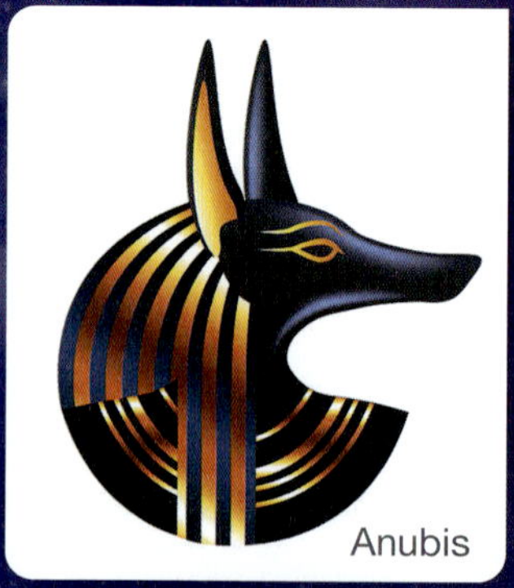
Anubis

No Sense of History

The ancient Egyptians had many names for their sky goddess. Nut, which means "sky" in the language of ancient Egypt, was one common name. Another, Mistress of All, grew from the belief that her body stretched over all of the earth's surface. The Egyptians pictured their sky goddess as a very large naked woman whose body arched across the heavens above. Indeed, her toes were said to be anchored somewhere, out of human sight, in the distant east; her tummy floated directly above, at the highest point in the sky; and her fingertips rested somewhere beyond the western horizon. People readily accepted that the reason her enormous body could not be seen was because she made herself invisible in order to hide her nakedness.

The goddess of the sky had at least one more name: She Who Protects. This was based on her physical relationship with the god of the sun, mighty Ra, frequently described as the leader of the Egyptian gods. It was widely accepted in some parts of Egypt that he was Nut's grandfather. Yet even though he was considerably older than she was, he needed her to replenish his shining body each day. Many Egyptians believed that just before dawn each day, Nut gave birth to Ra. After emerging from her womb, he passed over her arched body, traveling across the sky in a flying barge that held the sun's blindingly bright disk. Later, at dusk, the sun god maneuvered into Nut's mouth and made his way through her body and back into her womb. There he prepared to be reborn once again for the

RA
The Egyptian sun god, whom the sky goddess Nut was said to protect on a daily basis

dawning of a new day. Based on this regeneration of Ra each day, the sky goddess was seen as his protector; hence the nickname She Who Protects.

The general view among the ancient Egyptians was that Nut's protective powers extended well beyond Ra. It was commonly believed that she also protected the souls of the dead as they rose upward to become or mingle with the stars in the night sky. As a result, says history writer Kerry Sullivan,

> Nut came to be considered a protector of souls as they entered the afterlife. She was a friend to the dead, a mother-like guardian, who would help the souls leave the underworld and join her in the stars. For this reason, the inside lids of many sarcophagi [coffins] are painted with images of Nut. A prayer often written on ancient tombs reads "O my Mother Nut, stretch Yourself over me, that I may be placed among the imperishable stars which are in You, and that I may not die."[1]

GEB
The Egyptian god personifying the earth's surface; husband of the sky goddess Nut

Still another reason why Nut was so widely respected by the Egyptians was that, according to their stories, she gave birth to four of the most important of all Egyptian deities. She mated with her husband (who was also her brother) Geb, the god personifying the earth's surface. And this resulted in the birth of Isis, goddess of magic; Osiris, who eventually became ruler of the underworld; Nephthys, deity of water; and Seth, god of chaos and violence. In the eyes of the ancient Egyptians, producing such illustrious offspring made Nut a renowned mother goddess.

No Concept of Progress

One reason that Egyptians from each new generation told and retold the stories about Nut was the high degree of importance they

The sky goddess, pictured in the center of this image, had many names, including Nut, Mistress of All, and She Who Protects.

placed on those tales. Put simply, they did not view myths like the vast majority of people do today, as quaint, sometimes entertaining folklore. Rather, the ancient Egyptians believed wholeheartedly that Nut, along with other divine beings, was real and that at some time in the distant past she had actually done the things described in her myths.

Therefore, those legendary deeds, along with many others performed by Nut's fellow deities, were seen as important aspects of Egypt's history and world history in general. The reason for this was that the ancient Egyptians had no clear sense of history. Nor did they have a sense of social or scientific progress. They had no distinct conception of a society becoming progressively more advanced over time. As far as they could see, the world, and life within it, had been exactly the same since the gods had created it long before their own time.

One major consequence of this outlook on life was that there was no perceived need for formal written histories. In the words of the late, distinguished scholar H.W.F. Saggs, "With no concept of social progress," the Egyptians and other peoples of their era "had no incentive to make a conscious record of life in the thousand years before [their own time]."[2] The result was that no one thought to pen formal written histories to inform future generations of events in the past.

The Lives of a Vanished People

Another reason that the ancient Egyptians did not write their own histories was that they viewed their myths and history as one and the same. Their myths explained how the gods had fashioned the universe, including the earth's surface, the seas and lakes, the sky, and other aspects of nature. The myths also told how animals and humans had come to be. The collected myths essentially represented all that most ancient Egyptians needed or wanted to know about their past.

In addition, the myths provided people guidance in how to worship the gods, obey the king (in Egypt called the pharaoh), and live what was routinely seen as a proper life. In this way the collection of myths was viewed as a crucial, very much needed aspect of society and life in general. "Far from being a series of fossilized [accounts of] gods and goddesses," historian George Hart points out, many of those old tales "stand out as the projections of the ancient Egyptians' thoughts, hopes, and fears about the human condition and the troubles experienced in the course of one lifetime."[3] Therefore, an examination of those myths affords modern society a partial, fascinating window into the thoughts and lives of one of the most accomplished and influential of all ancient peoples.

CHAPTER ONE

How the World and People Came to Be

At first there was only an infinite expanse of water. There was no land at all, nor did any living things dwell within that limitless primordial sea. But this situation was not destined to exist forever. To this day no one can say for sure how it happened, but in some wonderfully miraculous manner, the mysterious and gifted god Ptah quite suddenly sprang into being and floated above the boundless ocean. From the start, he possessed the power of speech, and it was through that ability—the uttering of one command after another—that he began creating things. It was the power of Ptah's tongue, an ancient inscription states, that brought into being "all gods, all people, all cattle, all creeping things that live."[4]

PTAH
An Egyptian god who protected craftspeople and created the world through the spoken word

After setting the creation in motion, great Ptah decided he wanted help in that mighty endeavor. One of the first gods he "spoke" into being was Atum. Atum had inherited Ptah's driving urge to create meaningful things out of nothingness. As a result, Atum proceeded to create the first patch of dry land, the *ben-ben*. Standing upon it, he aided Ptah in carrying on the miraculous process of the creation.

So say the words carved into the Shabaka Stone. Dating from the late 700s BCE, that ancient text was a copy of a far older text created in ancient Egypt's first capital, Memphis, located 15 miles (24 km) south of modern-day Cairo. The original text summarized the creation account championed by the city's high priests. For that reason, it has come to be called the Memphite Theology.

Because these priests lived so long ago and left behind so few writings, it is difficult to know exactly why they chose to promote Ptah as the initial creator deity. However, modern Egyptologists and other scholars have made some educated guesses in that respect. The selection of Ptah, they suggest, may have been related to the fact that he was seen as the champion and protector of craftspeople and artists. Such individuals had an ability to do something that most other people could not. They could conceive of a useful or beautiful object and then, through talent and skill, create that object from various raw materials. The belief was that such special skills came from Ptah himself. It made sense, therefore, that this deity was the original creator of *all* things. Egyptologist James P. Allen summarizes what may have motivated the thinking of the Memphite priests:

> Crafts such as building and sculpture involve an initial concept in the artisan's mind. Eventually, through the artist's skill, this concept takes shape as a finished building, or a statue carved from stone. To the Memphite [priests], the link between the artist's concept and the ultimate transformation of his raw material was the force embodied by the god Ptah. Ptah's theologians united the two concepts of craftsmanship and the creative word into a single theory of creation.[5]

A Nation Favored by the Gods?

A tale such as the Memphite Theology—describing how the world and all things within it got started—is called a cosmogony. Although the cosmogony detailing Ptah's creation exploits was well known throughout ancient Egypt, so were three other major creation stories. One came from the city of Iunu (located where modern-day Cairo now stands), better known in later ages by

According to Egyptian myth, Ptah created all gods, people, and animals.

its Greek name—Heliopolis. Another cosmogony came from the town of Khemnu (located100 miles [161 km] south of Memphis), later better known by its Greek name, Hermopolis. And the fourth major creation story originated in the city of Thebes (lying a few hundred miles south of Hermopolis).

These four cosmogonies have certain similarities. All feature a primeval, infinite ocean, for example, and all four call the first land to appear within those waters the ben-ben. But the four stories also differ in certain respects, especially about which god or gods did the creating and exactly how. Moreover, some parts of the four creation accounts actually contradict one another. And yet the Egyptians accepted all four cosmogonies as equally valid.

The reason for this can be found in Egypt's ancient history. Before Egypt became a unified country under the first pharaoh, Narmer, in about 3100 BCE, each of the many Egyptian regions and towns worshipped a local deity or deities. Those gods, thought to oversee and protect the local people, were often different from the ones worshipped a mere hundred miles to the north or south. Similarly, a given region or town sometimes had its own creation myth, usually featuring the local protector god.

When Narmer eventually united all these regions and towns into a single nation, he recognized that selecting only one cosmogony and creator deity for everybody would likely cause widespread discontent. For the sake of maintaining order and loyalty, therefore, he wisely kept all the former gods and religious traditions. As scholar Leonard H. Lesko explains, "Gradually, or perhaps quickly, local myths from throughout the country were brought together into a system. . . . One cannot be sure how long it took to create this national mythology, which sought to include almost every god and thereby to satisfy almost every person. It was a product of genius, however, and laid the foundation for one of the longest-lived civilizations in history."[6]

In spite of the differences in the four creation stories, the fact that they had all become part of the national mythology was one

King Narmer, depicted in this carving, was Egypt's first pharaoh and unified the country.

Speech via the Heart or the Brain?

According to the Memphite creation tale, the god Ptah created things via the spoken word. That is, he either named or verbally described an object or living being, and within mere seconds that object or being materialized, seemingly out of nowhere. For example, a surviving stone carving found at Memphis quotes Ptah as saying that he created the deity Atum "from [my] tongue." Interestingly, the same inscription has Ptah say that Atum "came into being from [my] heart." Moreover, "every word of [mine] came into being through what the heart thought and the tongue commanded." At first glance, creating something via the heart appears to contradict the idea of creation through the tongue, or speech. However, Egyptologists point out that the word *heart* in the inscription does not mean the same thing it means today. The fact is that the Egyptians mistakenly believed that the heart, rather than the brain, is the seat of intelligence, thinking, and personality. As a result, it was also believed that the gods sometimes spoke to humans via the heart.

Quoted in Leonard H. Lesko, "Ancient Egyptian Cosmogonies and Cosmology," in Byron E. Shafer, ed., *Religion in Ancient Egypt*. Cornell University Press, 1991, p. 96.

reason the Egyptian people came to view them as equally acceptable. The other reason was the air of mystery surrounding the creation. The country's priests, regardless of which cosmogony they promoted, reminded the citizenry that the creation was so ancient that the exact facts surrounding it would likely always be unclear and perhaps even beyond human comprehension. According to this view, the important thing about the creation was that it had occurred in Egypt. And that made Egypt what later Latin writers would call the axis mundi, or center of the world. Therefore, the gods favored Egypt above all other nations and peoples.

Atum and the Sacred Ennead

Still another reason that the four differing creation stories seemed acceptable to average Egyptians was that some of those accounts combined elements from others. A prominent example was the Memphite cosmogony, in which Ptah created Atum, who then fashioned the first patch of land. This version of the creation essentially added Ptah and his contributions to another version in which Atum was the main creator deity.

Aten: Creation by Divine Desire

In addition to the four major creation stories—from Memphis, Heliopolis, Hermopolis, and Thebes—the ancient Egyptians recognized a few other, far less influential, myths relating to which gods made the world. From a modern viewpoint, the best known of those alternate creation tales was short lived but revolutionary for its time. That cosmogony was promoted by the pharaoh Akhenaten, who reigned around 1352 to 1336 BCE. A true maverick whose religious views were then seen as highly radical, he attempted to toss out the traditional gods and the myths associated with them. He insisted that they were all false and that there is only one, all-powerful god, called Aten. Akhenaten claimed that Aten is visible to everyone because that deity and the sun's blindingly bright disk are one and the same. Furthermore, the pharaoh said, Aten created all things through the tremendous power of his divine will. One of several hymns to Aten, which Akhenaten himself may have composed, addresses that god, saying, "You did create the world according to your desire, while you were alone. All men, cattle, and wild beasts, whatever is on earth, going upon its feet, and what is on high, flying with its wings. How manifold [diverse] it is, what you have made."

Quoted in Lionel Casson, *Daily Life in Ancient Egypt*. American Heritage, 1975, p. 99.

That Atum-centered cosmogony was the one endorsed by the priests at Iunu, or Heliopolis. They held that Atum abruptly and miraculously leaped into being from the dark depths of the original limitless sea. Part of an ancient hymn to Atum quotes him as saying, "I lifted myself from the watery mass." At that point, he goes on, "the earth had not come into being, [and] the creatures of the earth and the reptiles had not [yet] been made." Also, there was not yet any land for him to stand on. So, he says, "I laid a foundation," a reference to his creation of the ben-ben. Thereafter, Atum recalls, "I made every form [of living thing]."[7]

Among those living things, according to surviving ancient sources, were new gods. Some accounts claim that the first two deities Atum made were Shu, god of air, and his twin sister Tefnut, goddess of rain, dew, and other forms of moisture. In their turn, Shu and Tefnut then brought forth two more divine beings—the earth god Geb and sky goddess Nut. Wasting no time, Geb and Nut mated, and soon afterward Nut gave birth to Isis, Osiris, Nephthys, and Seth. Together, the Egyptians recognized Atum and his eight immediate offspring—Shu, Tefnut, Geb, Nut, and Nut's four children—as a sacred group of divinities called the Ennead.

Directly after the emergence of the Ennead, the Heliopolitan cosmogony claims, the ben-ben rapidly expanded, forming the world's mountains, valleys, plains, and forests. And next came the creation of humans. According to the Pyramid Texts, a series of tomb carvings produced in the late 2000s BCE, "Men and women arose from tears which came forth from [Atum's] eye."[8] Finally, according to the priests at Heliopolis, Atum made the diverse plants and animals that have existed in nature ever since.

A Monstrous Explosion

The nine-member Ennead was not the only primordial group of creator deities recognized by the ancient Egyptians. The third major creation story—advocated by the priesthood at Khemnu, or Hermopolis—also featured such a group. And the number of gods it contained was revealed in the town's name, because in Greek *Hermopolis* means "Town of the Eight." Those eight deities, collectively called the Ogdoad, were Amun, Amaunet, Nun, Naunet, Hey, Hauhet, Kek, and Kauket.

OGDOAD
According to the priests of Hermopolis, a group of eight gods said to have always existed

Although both the Heliopolitan and Hermopolitan creation accounts feature a core group of divinities, the manner in which their members came into being was very different. In the Ennead-centered version from Heliopolis, Atum suddenly appeared in the midst of the vast, dark primeval sea. He then proceeded to create the Ennead's other members. By contrast, in the Ogdoad-centered tale from Hermopolis, no divine being created the eight original gods. Instead, by some mysterious process that the local priests claimed was unknowable, the eight deities had somehow always existed in those endless, murky waters.

Another unique feature of the Hermopolitan creation story was the way it envisioned the eight gods' physical forms. Rather than having humanlike bodies, they looked like frogs, snakes, and other water-dwelling creatures. Furthermore, they navigated the limitless waters in pairs; Kek always swam alongside Kauket, for instance, and Nun remained at the side of Naunet.

In theory, the four pairs of gods might have continued to travel through the eternal ocean forever. But as the priests at Hermopolis told it, for reasons unknown they suddenly felt a mutual attraction none of them could resist. Abruptly, they merged and in the process underwent a tremendous transformation into a single, human-shaped divinity—the sun god Ra.

So powerful were the energies involved in Ra's formation that they unleashed a monstrous explosion that parted the waters and created the ben-ben, In George Hart's words:

> From the burst of energy released within the churned-up primal matter, the primeval mound was thrust clear. Its location later became Hermopolis, but its original emergence was described as the Isle of Flame because the sun-god was born on it and the cosmos witnessed the fiery glow of the first sunrise. It was the primacy of the Ogdoad in this cataclysmic event that seems to have been paramount in the Hermopolis myth.[9]

Amun-Ra, Khnum, and the Making of Humans

One of the eight deities from the Hermopolitan Ogdoad—Amun—also played a much larger role in the fourth major Egyptian cosmogony. The priests at Thebes, which rose to prominence as one of Egypt's leading cities in the 1500s BCE, asserted that Amun possessed a twofold character and personality that made him particularly special among the gods. In the Theban creation tale, Amun and Ra were one and the same being from the beginning. Indeed, as the mighty Amun-Ra, he existed *before* the

Ogdoad's other members did and went on to create them as well as the other deities the Egyptians worshipped. That made him in a sense the king of the gods, or least the most powerful and influential of their number.

AMUN-RA
In the Theban creation tale, the deity of the sun and leader of all the gods

Another reason that the Theban cosmogony—with Amun-Ra in its starring role—was so popular was that it claimed he instigated the creation of the human race. Supposedly, as he fashioned the various gods, he concluded that they deserved to have a race of mortal beings worshipping them. And part of that worship would take the form of providing the deities with gifts in the form of sacrifices of animals and plants.

But although Amun-Ra decided that the creation of people was necessary, he did not fashion humans himself. Instead, he assigned that task, along with the creation of animals, to a local Theban deity named Khnum, whom Egyptian artists depicted as a man with a ram's head. A talented divine craftsman and protector

Khnum formed men and women with clay from the banks of the Nile River.

of potters, the ram-headed deity eagerly set about his new job as the sun god's fellow creator. A surviving hymn to Khnum tells how he formed living things from the rich clay lining the banks of the Nile River. In addition to making cattle, fish, and other animals, it says, he also fashioned men and women. "He built the skull, formed the cheeks, to furnish shape to the image. He opened the eyes, hollowed out the ears, he made the body inhale air. He formed the mouth for eating [and] formed the tongue to speak."[10]

In ancient Egyptian eyes, whichever cosmogony one accepted, there was no denying that the creation had occurred in clear-cut stages. All had begun as a vast, dark sea. And from it there had arisen divine beings with an urge to produce more gods, as well as dry land, mountains, and forests. Finally, people and animals had emerged. And that had brought the grand cycle of creation to a memorable close.

CHAPTER TWO

A Vast Array of Immortal Beings

The ancient Egyptians had no trouble at all identifying Anubis, their god of mummification and one of the chief deities who oversaw the dead. Although his body was clearly humanoid—with a torso, two arms, and two legs—his head was that of a jackal. In some ways that seemed appropriate. After all, jackals are creatures that tend to feed by scavenging the meat of dead animals.

Anubis was said to be an offspring of the lord of the underworld, Osiris. Myths claimed that Osiris and his sister, Nephthys, mated and produced Anubis at a time when Nephthys was married to her brother Seth. And because Seth had a bad temper, she feared he would punish her harshly. Hence, she abandoned baby Anubis in a stretch of arid wilderness far from the well-watered Nile Valley.

ANUBIS
The god who oversaw the mummification of human bodies and the weighing of their souls in the afterlife

Somehow the infant survived for several days before Osiris's divine wife Isis, who was famous for her motherly instincts, found the baby and proceeded to raise him as her own child. As it turned out, that proved to be helpful for her in the years that followed. According to the prolific Greco-Roman writer Plutarch, "when the child had been found, after great toil and trouble . . . [he] was brought up and became her guardian and attendant . . . and it is said [that Anubis came] to protect the gods just as dogs protect men."[11]

Due in part to his connection with Osiris and the underworld, as an adult deity Anubis took charge of several important death rituals. One was mummification, the process in which a body was preserved after death by drying or embalming the flesh. It was thought that mummifying a corpse properly prepared and safeguarded the deceased's body and soul for the journey to the afterlife.

Another important death ritual that Anubis came to oversee was a special ceremony that took place when the gods examined a person's soul to see whether it was worthy of entering Osiris's subterranean realm. That ritual was called the Weighing of the Heart. First, Anubis took a human soul to a section of the underworld known as the Hall of Maat, named for the goddess who worked to maintain nature's balance. There, says Judy Aitken, curator of London's Cuming Museum, Anubis weighed the soul's heart "against the weight of a feather. If the heart and feather balanced then the dead person was judged to be good and passed into a happy eternity. If the heart outweighed the feather then it was judged to be heavy with guilt due to all the bad deeds the person had committed in life. That soul was then cast away to oblivion."[12]

Categorizing the Gods

While Anubis went about his regular duties as one of Egypt's death deities, many other gods carried out their own jobs and responsibilities. Osiris continued to oversee the vast underworld, for instance. Meanwhile, Ra made sure the sun moved across the sky each day; Nut continued to use her gigantic body to form the great dome of the sky; the cow-shaped Hathor oversaw joyfulness, music, and dance; Khnum made sure the Nile gently flooded each year, making agriculture possible; and Sekhmet guarded the pharaohs, particularly in wartime.

These beings made up only a tiny fraction of the many hundreds of deities recognized and worshipped by the Egyptians.

Anubis examines the balance in the Weighing of the Heart ritual.

In fact, after more than two centuries of intense study, modern scholars remain unsure how many of those gods there were in all. Even average ancient Egyptians, most of whom were illiterate and uneducated, had trouble keeping track of the numerous members of their divine pantheon (total collection of gods). Also daunting was trying to remember the seemingly countless stories about those deities and other supernatural beings.

Fortunately for ordinary Egyptians, they could rely on a class of authorities who variously recorded, recited, and explained those many myths. These experts were members of Egypt's large, literate, and politically powerful priesthood. Their crucial duties included maintaining the gods' temples, organizing religious festivals that celebrated those deities, and passing on the many myths to the next generation of Egyptians.

To make the diverse gods and their stories easier to remember and understand, the priests sorted and categorized them in various ways. Egyptologist David P. Silverman explains:

> Some deities became identified with the environment, some with the cosmos, some with creation, some with kingship, some even with humankind. In order to deal with the rapidly increasing number of higher beings, the Egyptians formulated a hierarchy for their gods. The gods were described, like mortals on earth, as living in a complex society, and as having separate family groupings.[13]

Beings Part Human and Part Animal

One such grouping of deities consisted of gods with both human and animal traits. Modern scholars describe those part-animal, part-human gods as zoomorphs. The jackal-headed god and master of mummification, Anubis, was one of the most beloved and widely respected members of that group.

THOTH
The Egyptian deity of wisdom, writing, and learning, who also protected scribes

Another important zoomorph in the Egyptian pantheon was Thoth, usually pictured with the body of a human male and head of an ibis, a water bird common in the ancient Nile Valley. It was thought that Thoth invented writing, magic, music, and medicine and that he possessed much wisdom. In addition, people believed that, aided by his divine wife Seshat, he managed a vast library created by the gods. According to myth, one of the most prominent books in that library was a volume he authored himself—the *Book of Thoth*. Supposedly, it contained secrets about the universe that only a few gods were privy to.

Another of Thoth's myths claims that he came to the aid of the goddess Nut and in so doing set the number of days in the year.

Protector of Childbirth

A good many Egyptian deities were protectors of people and the natural world. Among them was Bes, a god who provided protection for new mothers and their babies during childbirth. Bes is described here by Kyle Jordan, a curator at the Ashmolean & Pitt Rivers Museum in Oxford, England.

> Bes is depicted as a man of short stature—sometimes the result of a condition we refer to as dwarfism today—and as having strong muscles, a large belly, and a very expressive face. At one moment smiling with his tongue sticking out, and in another snarling and fearsome. . . . Sometimes naked and sometimes clothed with a kilt or leonine [lion-like] skin and a crown of plumed feathers, . . . [he] was also seen as a warrior and protector. He had a special responsibility for pregnant women, mothers and their infant children. In this guise, we typically find Bes with a snarling face, an assertive posture and a large knife raised in one hand. The Egyptians believed that he stood guard during childbirth, ready to strike any malevolent forces that sought to harm both mother and child.

Kyle Jordan, "Bes," Ashmolean Museum. www.ashmolean.org.

Long ago, the story goes, Ra forbade Nut from giving birth on any day of the year, which then had 360 days. Upset, Nut, who urgently wanted children, asked Thoth for help. Cleverly, he siphoned off some of the moon's light and with it created five more days, making the year 365 days long. That allowed Nut to have babies during the extra five days.

Other well-known Egyptian zoomorphs included the ram-headed Khnum, creator of humans, and Hathor, most often pictured as a cow. (When angry, she took the form of a lioness.) In Hathor's most popular myth, her usual joy transformed into rage. According to historian Evan Meeham, the tale "began with humanity making fun of Ra in his old age. Ever sensitive to insults, Ra sent his daughter Hathor to punish humans for their insolence. In the form of a lioness, she slaughtered all who dared to ridicule Ra. Ra eventually decided that the humans had been punished enough and called Hathor off. By this time, however . . . [he] could do nothing to stop her."[14]

The sun god had to resort to getting his daughter drunk to halt her rampage. Thereafter, as a playful jest, the other deities nicknamed Hathor the Lady of Drunkenness. Fortunately, she took no offense because, by then, she had regained her well-known sense of humor.

Gods of the Sky

Another group of gods oversaw the celestial objects that are visible in the daytime and nighttime skies. Of these, the god most often associated with the blindingly bright sun was Ra. Of his several myths, the best known depicts him riding in a big barge that traversed the sky each day carrying the sun's shining orb.

Meanwhile, another celestial deity, Khonsu, carried the moon's far less bright orb across the night sky. In his principal myth, he took the form of a bull that physically changed in size each month. When the moon was in its crescent stage, he was a small, young bull; later, during the full moon, he was an aged, overweight beast.

> **KHONSU**
> **The god who was thought to carry the moon's silvery orb across the night sky**

As for Nut, the Egyptians envisioned her not simply as the embodiment of the sky but also as a general overseer of the stars, planets, and other heavenly bodies. Ancient Egyptian artists illustrated that aspect of her myth by showing those objects either attached to or shining through her immense, arched body. It may be that the Egyptians also saw her as encompassing the Milky Way (the hazy band of light—made up of the glow of millions of stars in the center of our galaxy—that stretches across part of the night sky). UK-based astrophysicist Or Graur suggests that evidence for this can be seen in an ancient writing called the *Book of Nut*. In it, he points out, "Nut's head and rear are equated with the western and eastern horizons, respectively. Her arms, though, are described as lying at an angle to her body, with her right arm in the northwest and her left arm in the southeast. This very specific orientation is precisely that of the Milky Way in the winter sky."[15]

Ra, the sun god, carried the sun's shining orb across the sky each day.

A Protective Shield for Humanity

Still another group of gods was associated with various aspects of Egyptian society and the interactions, needs, and emotions of the people. Some of these deities protected the human race from evil and destructive beings and forces. One such protector, the goddess Taweret, guarded women during childbirth, while her fellow divinity Bes watched over children. Likewise, the god Kherty guarded human souls lying in tombs and graves.

At the same time, the force of love, when given to people by a god, was seen as an especially potent protective shield for humanity. And by far the most important and popular deity associated with love was Osiris's wife Isis. A symbol of motherhood and prolific dispenser of motherly love, her myths are filled with moral lessons about how people should treat one another with decency and respect.

One of the most widely retold stories is most often called "Isis and the Scorpions." It begins with that goddess traveling with her infant son Horus. Accompanying and guarding them were seven scorpions, each the size of a small horse. When the company reached a village in the Nile Delta, the weary and hungry goddess knocked on the door of the biggest, finest house in town. She hoped the owner would be kind enough to offer food and a place to rest. Instead, the woman who answered the door called Isis a filthy beggar and demanded she leave. Disappointed, Isis next came to a small, rickety shack. Its owner, a poor fisher, welcomed the strangers and gave them food.

Angered by the rich woman's refusal to help, one of the scorpions returned to her house and stung her small son. When the boy fell seriously ill, his mother ran through the village pleading for help. To her surprise, the first person who offered to help was the beggar she had so rudely turned away. Except now the woman learned that the beggar was no beggar at all but the goddess Isis. Despite the woman's earlier rude behavior, the kindly goddess refused to let an innocent child suffer and die. Isis revealed her true identity to all the village's residents. According to a surviving ancient document, she said, "I am Isis the goddess, Mistress of Magic, who makes magic, glorious of speech." Picking up the ail-

Heqet: Protector of New Life

The goddess Heqet was one of the most revered deities in ancient Egypt. Her core duty was to oversee and protect fertility, both of the soil and of animal and human reproduction. In particular, she came to be closely associated with childbirth, and pregnant women regularly prayed to her. People believed that she helped ensure that mother and baby would safely make it through the birth process and early infancy.

Heqet also played a key role in another fertility-related aspect of Egyptian life—the gentle annual flooding of the Nile River, which provided the water necessary to irrigate farmers' crops. Her divine husband Khnum oversaw the yearly floods. The ancient Egyptians believed that Heqet assisted her mate in that process. Thus, Egyptian society came to rely on her as a protector of new life—in the form of healthy infants and the crops needed to sustain the nation's growing population.

Isis (right) was the wife of Osiris (left), and a symbol of motherhood and love. Here, she is holding her infant son, Horus.

ing child, she employed her divine powers, chanting, "[Poison] be powerless, be repulsed, retreat, flee back, poison!"[16]

Thanks to Isis, the child quickly regained his health, and his mother learned a powerful lesson. After thanking the goddess, she gathered her jewels and gold coins and gave them away to the poorest of her neighbors. She had learned the value of hospitality and common decency—values shared by the people of ancient Egypt and reinforced by their many myths.

CHAPTER THREE

Death and Transfiguration on the Nile

Although in real life, Narmer was Egypt's first pharaoh, the Egyptians believed the myth claiming that two gods—Osiris and Horus—ruled the country before the reign of Narmer. In the story told in the myth, when the divine Osiris entered his throne room one evening to attend a dinner party, the last thing on his mind was his own death. Nor was he thinking about transfiguration, or the miraculous conversion of a lifeless corpse into a new living being. All he wanted that evening was to enjoy a good meal and the pleasant company of family and friends. Certainly, the pharaoh did not realize that his own brother was about to murder him. (In his heavenly form, Osiris was immortal. But in his earthly form, which he had taken to serve as Egypt's king, his body could die.)

In fact, by the time Osiris entered the room, that event had already been set in motion. Osiris's brother and chief advisor, the god Seth, had long been jealous of his more illustrious brother. Osiris and his queen, the goddess Isis, had proved to be excellent rulers who cared about all Egyptians, including the poorest farmers and laborers. So it was not surprising that people from all walks of life frequently thanked and praised them. This devotion greatly irritated Seth, who was by nature insecure and resentful. For these reasons, Seth conceived a plan to slay his brother and seize the nation's throne.

He waited until Isis, who was both smart and powerful, was away from the capital to set his scheme in motion. With her out of the way, he invited various government officials and nobles to

SETH
The god of violence and chaos, who slew his own brother, Osiris

the palace for a feast, supposedly to honor the pharaoh. Making a grand entrance, Seth was followed by several of his servants, who carried a big, well-decorated box about the size of a coffin. After everyone had eaten, Seth told those gathered that he had devised a parlor game they were sure to enjoy. He explained that each player would climb into the decorated box, and the individual whose body fit inside the best would be awarded possession of the elegant container. One by one, the guests climbed inside, but no one's body exactly conformed to its dimensions.

Then it was the pharaoh's turn. Smiling, Osiris lay down inside the box, and sure enough, his body was a perfect it. There was a round of polite applause, and when it concluded the ruler began to climb out. But suddenly, to the surprise of all present, Seth grabbed hold of the box's lid and slammed it shut, trapping the king inside. As the guests watched in horror, Seth's servants quickly drove nails into the lid. Then, as the late University of Southern California scholar Norma L. Goodrich told it, they "poured molten lead all along the joints, thus sealing it hermetically. Within a few minutes, they knew that Osiris had smothered to death. Then, as previously arranged, they carried the chest to the bank of the Nile and heaved it into the water. As they watched the current catch it and carry it swiftly downstream, the triumphant Seth realized that he was the ruler of Egypt."[17]

Salvation for Everyone

Osiris's murder by his brother is the opening episode in a sprawling, complex, dramatic story in which the dead king is eventually resurrected. Modern scholars have come to call it the Myth of Kingship. Of the more than one thousand separate myths the ancient Egyptians recognized, they viewed this one as the most crucial and compelling. Part of its importance stemmed from the

ISIS
Egypt's leading goddess of motherhood, who used her potent magic to reassemble the pieces of her dead husband's body

fact that its four main characters were among the most powerful and influential gods in the country's divine pantheon. Osiris, Isis, and Seth were members of the sacred Ennead, the group of nine gods whose worship was centered at Heliopolis. And the Egyptians saw the fourth major player in the myth—Horus, son of Osiris and Isis—as a hero and religious figure of epic proportions.

Beyond that, the tale helped ordinary people understand the origins of Egypt's many rulers, all of whom were believed to be gods. People came to believe that when a pharaoh died, his soul literally

Seth tricked Osiris into lying down in the chest, and then he quickly closed it and nailed it shut.

Resurrection: A Core Belief

The ancient Egyptians strongly believed in the resurrection of human souls following death. In *Ancient Egypt: Everyday Life in the Land of the Nile*, historians Bob Brier and Hoyt Hobbs comment on how the Myth of Kingship reflected this belief.

> No civilization invested more faith, energy, or money in attaining life after death than ancient Egypt. Its people loved life, but made extensive and costly preparations for death because their religion promised they would live again—just as the myth of Isis and Osiris taught. . . . [That story] contains their most basic beliefs about death. Even the box that fit Osiris later became their [standard] human-shaped coffin. [The myth] demonstrates the Egyptians' most important religious belief: resurrection—that a physical body would literally revive in the next world, just as Osiris was magically reanimated. To gain a perfect eternal life required an intact body. Isis went to such lengths to retrieve the corpse of her husband for a proper burial because, if she had not pieced together his dismembered body, the available vehicle for eternal life, he could not have been resurrected.

Bob Brier and Hoyt Hobbs, *Ancient Egypt: Everyday Life in the Land of the Nile*. Sterling, 2009, pp. 53–54.

merged, or become one, with that of Osiris. Thus, that mighty deity was seen not only as the overseer of the realm of the dead but also as a mystical blending of the souls of Egypt's national leaders.

The Myth of Kingship had an important spiritual dimension as well. In Egypt's earliest centuries, before this myth took hold, it was assumed that only the pharaoh enjoyed an existence in the afterlife and that ordinary people had nothing to look forward to after death. After the story of Osiris's transfiguration became widespread, however, that view changed. The ancient Egyptians came to believe that Osiris's resurrection ensured salvation and entry into the afterlife for all people—from the poorest laborers to the loftiest nobles. "It was not the earthly role of Osiris that was significant," George Hart explains, "but the miracle of his resurrection from death, offering the hope of a community of existence for everyone in the underworld."[18]

The First Mummy

These profound religious and social ideas about death and the salvation of human souls began to develop well after 2500–2400 BCE, the period when the myth of Osiris's death and subsequent resurrection first appeared in Egypt. In that eventful story, in the weeks and months following Osiris's murder, the Egyptian people did not envision that the dead king might somehow come back to life. Even Isis, who was horrified to learn of his death on her return to the capital, was at first concerned only with retrieving his body. And she launched an intensive search for it. In time she found the box that had become his coffin lying at the bottom of one of the Nile's many tributaries. Hoping to keep Seth and his henchmen from getting their hands on it, she hid it in a nearby marsh.

By coincidence, however, a few days later Seth and some of his nobles went hunting in that very marsh and stumbled upon the box. Seth was angry that someone—most likely Isis, he guessed—had pulled the box from the river, and he ordered some of his guards to cut Osiris's corpse into hundreds of pieces and hide them all over the country. Clearly, the new king assumed that this move would foil his sister's attempt to give the body a decent burial.

But Seth had totally underestimated the intensity of Isis's love for her husband and her sheer resourcefulness. In Plutarch's words, she searched ceaselessly "through the swamps in a boat of papyrus" and one by one found every piece of the body. Then, to honor Osiris, Plutarch added, she "held a funeral for each [body] part when she had found it."[19]

After that, Isis, assisted by her sister Nephthys, carefully pieced together the fragments of the dead pharaoh's corpse. That included wrapping it in linen strips, in the process creating the first mummy in Egypt's history. (Mummification and several other Egyptian funerary beliefs and customs originated in this story.)

Having embalmed Osiris's remains, it suddenly occurred to Isis that she might be able to employ her considerable magical abilities to bring him back to life. Indeed, after she had applied over a dozen

Isis mourns Osiris. After he died, she searched for his body, and after finding it at the bottom of the river, she hid it in a nearby marsh.

strong spells, her husband's body began to move. Within a few hours he had regained full consciousness. So happy were the two at being reunited that they proceeded to conceive a child together. At that moment, no one foresaw that the infant—a boy—was fated to play a crucial role in their continuing difficulties with Seth.

Osiris's Hidden Kingdom

Isis and Osiris remained in hiding for a few months after their son's birth. During that period, the resurrected former pharaoh decided it would be best if he no longer mingled with ordinary people. He feared that his presence as a reanimated corpse might frighten them. He decided to discuss the matter with the

The Edfu Pageant

The battles between Horus and Seth in the Myth of Kingship inspired an elaborate pageant, or play, staged each year in early January. It took place at the Temple of Horus at Edfu, a town located about 62 miles (100 km) south of Thebes. The celebration seems to have featured actors playing Horus and Seth, along with numerous extras in minor roles. Scenes from that dramatic presentation, which were carved into slabs of clay, have survived. In them, Seth is typically depicted as an angry hippo. Horus is shown in a boat, along with helpers—perhaps soldiers—hunting his nefarious uncle to get revenge on him for killing Osiris. Ten times Horus hurls a harpoon that pierces the Seth-hippo's hide. Arguably the most dramatic of those scenes is one in which Horus jumps onto the Seth-hippo's back and stabs him in the head. During these encounters, Horus wears the double crown of Upper and Lower Egypt, indicating that he is the rightful pharaoh, whereas Seth is nothing more than an illegal usurper.

chief god, Ra, who agreed that his fears were warranted. However, Ra had an idea. Because Osiris had undergone death and transfiguration, Ra said, he was now uniquely qualified to take on the job of ruler of the underworld.

In assuming control of that underground realm, Osiris told Ra that he did not want it to be a place of punishment. There would be rigorous initial tests to determine whether the souls of the dead were worthy of entrance into that land of eternal life, Osiris said. But once a person passed those tests, they would find the afterlife quite similar to life on the earth's surface.

Thus, writes historian Rosalie David, Osiris's hidden kingdom ended up being a well-watered, green expanse of forests, mountains, and valleys, close to a "mirror image of the cultivated land of Egypt." Sometimes called the Field of Reeds, David adds, its residents "were believed to enjoy eternal springtime, unfailing harvests, and no pain or suffering. The land was democratically divided into equal plots that rich and poor alike were expected to cultivate."[20]

The Powers of Love, Decency, and Justice

As the years progressed, practically all Egyptians came to look upon Osiris, lord of the Field of Reeds, with great awe and ad-

HORUS
Son of Osiris and Isis, he defeated Seth, thereby attaining revenge for Osiris's murder

miration. One of the few who saw him in a negative light was, not surprisingly, his brother Seth, who still sat on Egypt's throne. The bitter pharaoh remained enormously jealous of Osiris's popularity. But at least, Seth reasoned, he could rest easy knowing that neither Osiris nor Isis had sought vengeance for his past actions. This led the pharaoh to conclude that he might hold the throne for a long time to come.

In this hope for the future, Seth was sorely mistaken. His brother and sister had decided to refrain from getting revenge on him. But what Seth had failed to foresee was that the child they had conceived in the marshes years before—Horus by name—was now fully grown and very eager to avenge the wrongs Seth had inflicted on his parents. The young god began attacking his despicable uncle in hopes of toppling him from the throne.

Seth took the form of a hippopotamus and fought with Horus. Here, Horus spears the hippo.

In turn, Seth angrily accepted the challenge, and in the weeks that followed, he and Horus fought several times. In one clash, as the other gods watched, the two engaged in combat on the Nile's bank. Each plunged into the water and assumed the form of a gigantic, furious hippo. Hours passed, and still they fought relentlessly, each drawing much blood from the other. In a later battle, Seth gouged out Horus's eyes, but fortunately for Horus, the bovine goddess Hathor swiftly intervened and restored his sight.

Such fights continued for weeks until one day, seemingly out of nowhere, Osiris abruptly appeared and stood between them. As his powerful voice reverberated across the land, he delivered a warning to Seth. If he did not relinquish the kingship to Horus at once, Osiris would unleash upon Seth hundreds of hideous, bloodthirsty creatures that inhabited the darkest holes beneath the earth. Hearing this threat, Seth suddenly froze in abject fear. Aware that the scary creatures Osiris had mentioned were very real, he surrendered and gave up the throne to Horus.

Many Egyptians were surprised when, less than a year later, the heroic Horus abdicated the kingship and passed it on to the first of a long line of human rulers. In so doing, he explained that he had no serious desire to rule; rather, he had fought so long and hard primarily to get justice for his divine parents. Thereafter, as long as ancient Egypt existed, its residents deeply respected and worshipped the divine family comprising Osiris, Isis, and Horus. They had revealed the amazing powers of love, decency, and justice, as well as given all Egyptians hope for resurrection and survival following death. And for these gifts, the Egyptians were forever grateful.

CHAPTER FOUR

Marauding Monsters and Mayhem

The powerful and widely respected Egyptian Pharaoh Ramses II was extremely pleased by a special gift he had received from the ruler of Bakhtan, a small realm lying many miles northeast of Egypt. That gift was the ruler's daughter, who was beautiful, intelligent, kind, and a talented singer. Ramses was so happy with her that he made her one of his several wives. After only a year, he went further and gave her the honor of becoming his principal spouse, who thereafter bore the title of Queen of Egypt.

Seeking the Help of the Gods

A few months later a messenger arrived from Bakhtan with troubling news. The queen's sister, Princess Bentresh, was seriously ill. Her doctors could find no treatment for her illness, prompting her father to seek help from Ramses. He requested that Ramses send his best doctor to try to cure the sick princess. The pharaoh was genuinely concerned and immediately sent an Egyptian physician to Bakhtan. Riding the swiftest camel that could be found, the young doctor traveled nearly day and night, making his way through many deep forests, sweltering deserts, and rugged mountain ranges.

When the physician finally arrived in Bakhtan, the king greeted him and led him to Princess Bentresh's bedside. Examining her, the physician found that she had a high fever and that she did not recognize her own father, nor any of her other relatives and friends. After ruling out one disease after another, the physician determined that her condition was caused by a demon that had seized possession of her body. Repeatedly, the young man tried to drive the creature away, but all these efforts failed. The only remedy that might work, the physician told the king, was to ask Ramses to send one of the Egyptian gods to confront the demon.

When Ramses learned of that request, he wasted no time in asking the moon deity Khonsu for aid. Happy to help, the god traveled at top speed to Bakhtan. The very instant he reached the princess's bedside, he detected the demon, who in turn recognized him and was plainly afraid. The two now fought fiercely for almost an hour, and during that period young Bentresh wavered back and forth on the verge of death.

BENTRESH
The foreign woman who is possessed by a demon in the myth "The Princess and the Demon"

Eventually, the hawk-headed Khonsu defeated the demon, which became visible to onlookers when it fled the young woman's fever-wracked body. Its eyes were huge and yellow, and its misshapen torso was covered with blisters and poisonous insects. The twisted thing begged the god not to wipe it from existence. And after considering the matter, Khonsu agreed to spare the creature on the condition that it leave Bakhtan and never return. To the relief of all present, the demon agreed to the deal and hurriedly left the country.

Later that day, Princess Bentresh's overjoyed father sent word to Egypt that his daughter had been healed. Not long afterward he dispatched a caravan containing many luxurious gifts to Ramses's palace. When the pharaoh learned that his wife's sister had fully recovered, he rejoiced and ordered that all Egyptians send prayers of thanks to mighty Khonsu.

Fear of the Unknown

The widely popular tale of Khonsu's healing of Bentresh is most often called "The Princess and the Demon." It is only one of many

The moon deity Khonsu, depicted here, rushed to help Princess Bentresh and eventually defeated the demon that had taken possession of her body.

dozens of Egyptian myths that describe marauding monsters that usually (though not always) cause mayhem of various kinds. These often repugnant, scary beings were thought to exist alongside the gods, most of whom were seen as benevolent.

The ancient Egyptians widely accepted the existence of these mystical creatures and monsters as real. Although a monster might suddenly appear almost anywhere, most people believed they dwelled in the less accessible, wilder regions of Egypt. In particular, these included the expansive, arid, and rocky deserts lying beyond the lushly green Nile Valley. These were the places where a majority of sightings of such creatures occurred.

That ancient Egypt's supernatural creatures were seen as living in the regions lying beyond the bounds of civilization was not an accident. Culturally speaking, this belief spoke to the Egyptians' overall general view of themselves as compared to other peoples. The common belief was that the Egyptians were the most worthy and civilized human beings who existed anywhere. Accordingly, they envisioned that most or all of the lands lying beyond Egypt were largely disordered, dangerous places populated by barbarians.

In the Egyptian national consciousness, therefore, the desert was viewed not just as a remote, waterless, inhospitable area. It also symbolized the vast, unwelcoming world lying outside safe, nurturing Egypt. As a result, the uncivilized, often creepy creatures thought to inhabit the deserts symbolized the equally uncivilized, possibly hostile humans who lived beyond Egypt's borders. In both cases, the Egyptians' images of and thoughts about the remote desert portions of their country were colored by a general fear of the unknown.

The Biggest Category of Monsters

This fear of, or at least worry about, the uncivilized peoples and creatures lurking in faraway places is well illustrated by the events described in "The Princess and the Demon." The main setting is the distant land of Bakhtan, where even the king's daughter is not safe from demons. And only when the pharaoh and one of the gods of far more civilized Egypt intervene is the demon driven away.

That is not to say that Egypt itself was not sometimes plagued by demons. In fact, of all the categories of Egyptian monsters, that of demons was the biggest. Modern studies of ancient Egypt's surviving literary texts have revealed over four thousand references to demons. Not all of these creatures were seen as inherently evil or murderous. Egyptologist Kasia Szpakowska points out that some Egyptian demons were similar to the genies in Arabian folklore. "They would come to one's aid," she writes, "as often as they acted as fearsome, dangerous creatures."[21]

Were Griffins Real Creatures?

Many strange and often dangerous hybrid creatures were thought to lurk in Egypt's arid wilderness areas. Only a few included the serpopard, with the body of a leopard and head of a snake; babi, a bloodthirsty cross between a man and a baboon; and the bizarre sha, a blend of anteater, donkey, and jackal. Particularly colorful was the griffin, with a lion's body and an eagle's head and wings. Griffins also appear in the mythologies of several other ancient peoples, including the Greeks, Persians, and Assyrians. The Egyptians believed that griffins could be dangerous to traders and other travelers passing through the desert. In an alternate depiction, Egyptian griffins, like dragons in the myths of the Greeks, Germans, and Norse, guarded large hordes of treasure. Some modern scientists have suggested that the legend of the griffin was based on the skeletons of a medium-sized dinosaur called protoceratops. Supposedly, the ancients who found those remains assumed they belonged to a still-existing creature. Other experts, however, feel that the striking physical similarities between griffins and the protoceratops are coincidental and that griffins were purely mythical. That debate continues.

Nevertheless, a majority of Egyptian demons were quite monstrous and dangerous. Most often they had vile, horrifying bodies that combined features of two, three, or more animals. Common among those animals were reptiles (particularly snakes), cats, wolves, baboons, goats, donkeys, hippos, scorpions, insects, and vultures.

As for what motivated demons, some were pests that wandered from place to place and enjoyed inhabiting people's bodies, spreading dread diseases, and causing other sorts of misery. The demon in "The Princess and the Demon" appears to be one of those wandering demons. These malicious beings, like most demons, were invisible to human eyes. Therefore, they could be carried from town to town by the winds, completely unnoticed by their human victims.

In a fascinating twist, however, some other demons were actually sanctioned by certain gods and aided those deities in various ways. In one well-known myth, for example, Sekhmet, goddess of chaos, plagues, and war, commanded many demonic assistants who at her orders inflicted illnesses of diverse kinds on

BONE-SMASHER

One of Osiris's demonic assistants who devoured the souls of people judged unworthy to enter the afterlife

unfortunate people. And perhaps the most famous myth of this kind involved the demonic creatures that played roles in the post-death religious rituals in which people's souls attempted to reach the afterlife. After a person died, Osiris judged whether their soul was worthy of entering the underworld. If judged unworthy, the soul became a meal for one or more of the demonic assistants, who were at times collectively called "soul-swallowers." Individually, they had names such as Bone-Smasher, Blood-Eater, and Fiend from the Slaughterhouse. Worst of all was Ammut, the so-called Devourer of the Dead, which had a crocodile's head, a lion's front legs, and the rear end of a hippo.

Ammut had the head of a crocodile, the front legs of a lion, and the rear end of a hippo.

A Ceremony to Drive Away Apep

The monster Apep's daily attacks on the sun god's barge represented a grave threat to humanity. If Apep succeeded in disrupting the sun's rise, the world would become uninhabitable. So Egyptian priests developed a ceremony intended to help Ra and the other gods foil the monster. That ceremony was called the Banishing of Apep. In its initial stage, priests at each participating temple fashioned an effigy (model) of the beast. Next, they placed that image in the structure's center and fervidly prayed that all of Apep's evil traits would pass into the effigy. After that, the priests and their assistants violently attacked the effigy. They spat on it, beat it with wooden clubs, stabbed it with knives and swords, and finally burned it to ashes. The belief was that this ritual would help reduce the monster's powers and possibly even force it to leave Egypt for weeks, months, or longer.

The Ferocious Apep

Demons were by no means the only frightening creatures that toyed with humans and gods alike. In the sky, for instance, dwelled one of the most famous monsters of all. That monster, a giant, ferocious snakelike being known as Apep, repeatedly tried to thwart the son god, Ra. Each morning, as Ra mounted his glowing barge to carry the sun across the sky, Apep appeared seemingly out of nowhere. Hundreds of feet long, the beast frequently launched its attack when the glowing barge was passing over Bakhu Mountain, which the Egyptians believed held up the eastern portion of the sky.

But no matter where the assault took place, the creature's strategy was always the same. For reasons that remain unclear, it hated Ra and sought to overturn the barge and slay the god. One major difficulty for Ra was that taking the time to fight the monster would have interfered with the task of transporting the sun across the sky. Hence, the god assigned the task of defending the barge to one of the protector deities who regularly accompanied him. Numerous ancient versions of this myth survive, and they do not all agree on who rode in the barge and which god fought Apep. In some versions, Seth, brother of Osiris and Isis, jumped out and battled the great serpent. As told in an ancient inscription, while engaging it, Seth shouted, "Back, fiend, from the onslaught of

Ra fights Apep. This creature continually tried to overturn Ra's barge and kill him.

[Ra's] light!" And after delivering various threats, he added, "[Go] away, Apep, O enemy of Ra!"[22]

A number of other gods were also credited with fighting Apep, including Thoth and Isis. But the deity who supposedly actually managed to slay the beast was Bastet. Ra's daughter and a cat goddess who was often pictured as a powerful lioness with extremely sharp claws, she was said to have often ridden in the solar barge. According to Nitten Nair, creator of the online mythology site MythLok, Bastet used her "claws and teeth to fight off Apep and protect her father from this ambush. She would also use her magical powers to create spells and charms that would weaken Apep and make him vulnerable."[23] Eventually, one of Bastet's myths claims, her claws tore the monster to pieces.

Visitations by Ghosts

Average Egyptians enjoyed hearing stories about Apep and other monsters opposed by the gods, because they were entertaining and because demons like these had little interest in humans. This was not the case with an array of other menacing creatures.

Among them were giant baboon-like beasts, griffins (which were half eagle and half lion), and ghosts.

Ghosts were especially troubling for Egypt's human inhabitants. Surviving lore indicates that the spirits of the dead sometimes haunted and created problems for the living. In one surviving tale, a man is haunted by his deceased wife, who both scares him and makes him miserable. He continually pleads with her to leave him alone, saying that he always treated her well and therefore does not deserve to be tormented. "I did not divorce you and I did not injure your heart," he points out. "I did not hide anything from you during your life. I did not make you suffer pain in anything I did with you as your husband."[24] Regrettably, the story does not say whether the ghost stopped haunting the man.

Ghosts were apparently not always dangerous or scary, however. Some visited the living because they were lonely. Others set out to complain that too few relatives and friends had been visiting their graves. This is the case with the spirit in perhaps the best-known ancient Egyptian ghost story, sometimes called "Khonsemhab and the Ghost." In it, Khonsemhab, a high priest, is visited by the ghost of a man named Nebusemekh. When Khonsemhab asks what the spirit wants, it replies that it is very sad that over many years its tomb has fallen into ruin. Sympathetic to the ghost's plight, Khonsemhab promises he will try to refurbish the tomb. But what if the priest cannot deliver on that promise? Nebusemekh asks. In that case, the priest says, he will find ten servants—five male and five female—who will make sacrifices at the grave site on a regular basis.

KHONSEMHAB
An Egyptian high priest who encounters a ghost in a popular surviving myth

The story, written on pottery shards discovered by archaeologists, ends there because other pieces of the pottery were never found. So it is not known whether the priest ever made good on his promise. More certain is that he was fortunate he had not been visited by a soul-swallower, a demon, or one of the other fearsome monsters the Egyptians believed roamed their world.

CHAPTER FIVE

Famous Human Adventurers and Travelers

The daring young adventurer Setna was fortunate to have been born into Egypt's royal family. As one of the sons of the powerful Pharaoh Ramses II, he had the funds and political clout that most ordinary Egyptians lacked. That allowed the young man to involve himself in whatever public or private endeavors caught his fancy. Thus, when he heard a rumor about a lost tomb containing a lost book filled with secrets of magic, he became determined to find both the tomb and the book. With the aid of his brother Inaros, Setna spent several months searching for the tomb and finally found it.

A Family of Ghosts

As the two royal princes entered the dark, dusty crypt, they realized that the contents had remained untouched since it had been sealed centuries before. They also saw the name of the tomb's owner—a man named Naneferkaptah—written on one wall. There were also three coffins occupying the center of the main chamber. Searching further, Setna came upon a very old book resting on a stone pedestal. Inaros exclaimed that it must be the volume of magical spells they were seeking.

His eyes lighting up, Setna reached for the book, but before he could grasp it a deep, gravelly voice demanded that he stop. The brothers turned to see three semitransparent human forms, apparently ghosts, standing beside the caskets. One of the specters stepped forward and identified

NANEFERKAPTAH

The deceased man whose tomb the young Egyptian adventurer Prince Setna tries to rob

himself as Naneferkaptah. He introduced the others as his wife Ahwere and their son Merib and then told Setna that he had no right to take the book. That artifact belonged to the family, the apparition said. Then Ahwere spoke up, saying that she and her husband and son had died because of the book. According to historian Joshua J. Mark's telling of the myth, she recalled that Naneferkaptah, once a leading scribe, had made the mistake of stealing the book, "which was handwritten by the god Thoth himself, from a secret hiding place in the sea and Thoth, enraged, drowned first her son, then herself, and Naneferkaptah then drowned himself in grief."[25]

Defying the spirits, Setna seized the book and ran. He and his brother fled the tomb, slammed its outer door shut, and hurried to

Ramses II, pictured here hunting in his chariot, was the father of the daring young adventurer Setna.

the nearby city of Memphis. There, during the third night following his arrival, Setna had a strange, disturbing dream. In it, he was an older man with several children whom he loved dearly. As the dream continued, Setna suddenly fell madly in love with a beautiful woman and repeatedly offered her anything she wanted if she would marry him. The woman demanded that he hand over all his possessions, which he did. Then she slew his children and threw their bodies onto a crowded city street. Finally, Setna dreamed that he too was lying helpless in that street.

Waking up with a start, Setna realized it had only been a dream. His father Pharaoh Ramses was standing beside his son's bed and said that he had heard about how Setna had stolen the book from the tomb. Perhaps, Ramses said, the nightmare was sent by a god to punish the young man and scare him into returning the object to the tomb. Overcome by a wave of regret, Setna returned the book to Naneferkaptah's tomb. The young man also made sure the outer door was tightly sealed in hopes of keeping any future robbers from getting in.

Adventure and Escape

Like the story about Setna, myths that revolved around the exploits of people rather than gods or other supernatural beings appealed to the ancient Egyptians. The average person worked hard and had little opportunity for variety or excitement. These stories provided a sense of adventure, escape, and entertainment that could not be found in daily life.

Myths involving travel were particularly fascinating to ordinary Egyptians. This was because most of them never ventured beyond their own home regions, let alone to other countries. Indeed, wrote the late scholar of ancient Egypt Lewis Spence, the ancient Egyptians "were by no means travelers, and for the most part confined their journeys and excursions to the precincts of their own country." Over time, he says, a few merchants and soldiers did go to other lands. And when they re-

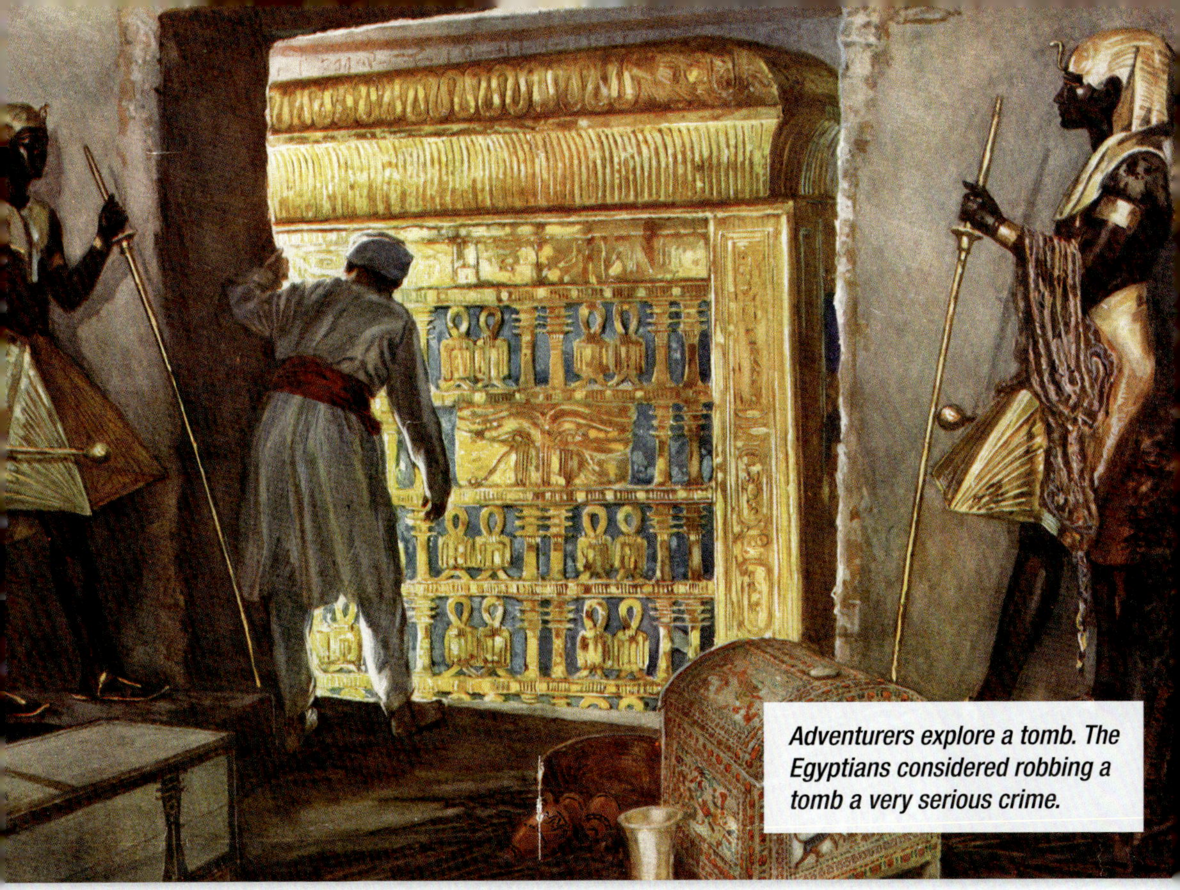

Adventurers explore a tomb. The Egyptians considered robbing a tomb a very serious crime.

turned home, it was customary for them "to gather their friends and neighbors about them and regale them with an account of their travels."[26]

Another factor that made these stories popular and enduring was that, beyond their sheer entertainment value, they frequently taught listeners moral or cultural lessons. For example, the tale of Setna's search for the book, Mark points out,

> conveys a number of important cultural values. Tombs were considered the eternal homes of the dead and tomb robbing was a very serious crime. . . . [Curses were often written] on tomb walls, promising vengeance on any who would desecrate or steal from the deceased. The fact that Setna, identified as a prince . . . is punished for [stealing the book] would have made it clear that no one is exempt from eternal justice.[27]

The Diplomat, the Sailor, and the Snake

One of ancient Egypt's most famous myths combines entertainment value with the main character's learning of important lessons about life. Titled "The Shipwrecked Sailor," it begins with an Egyptian government official—a diplomat—pacing back and forth on the deck of a vessel on its way home from a trip to a foreign land. After a while, a wealthy, well-dressed man asked the diplomat why he was pacing so much. The diplomat answered that his mission to make a deal with a foreign ruler had failed, and he was worried that the pharaoh might be angry and punish him. The rich man smiled and urged him not to fret. Sometimes what seems negative can end up being positive, he said. And to prove that, he told the diplomat his own story.

Years before, the wealthy man began, he had been a poor young sailor. One day a violent storm had struck his vessel, and he had found himself shipwrecked and alone on an uncharted island. He assumed that for the rest of his life he would be lonely and miserable. But after exploring for a while, he discovered that he was not alone after all, for a large snake dwelled there too.

The Eloquent Peasant

Myths about ordinary people who eventually became accomplished or famous were told and retold for centuries in ancient Egypt. These included tales of adventurers, like Setna, and travelers, such as Sinuhe. Another popular myth in that category was most often called "The Story of the Eloquent Peasant." It begins with a poor farmer, Khun-Anup, carrying what little food he has grown to market. On the way, he passes through the property of a wealthy landowner named Nemtynakht, who beats Khun-Anup and steals his goods. In a haughty tone, Nemtynakht tells his victim that he has no recourse because no one will take the word of a lowly peasant over that of a respected landowner. However, Khun-Anup is determined to get justice. He goes to a magistrate in a nearby town and recounts what happened. The magistrate advises Khun-Anup to write down the reasons why he deserves justice and is surprised by how beautifully written the document is. It is so eloquent, in fact, that other high-placed people, including the pharaoh, end up seeing it. The pharaoh is so moved by it that he orders Nemtynakht's estate to be confiscated and given to the overjoyed peasant.

The creature, which incredibly possessed the ability to talk, was friendly and explained that it had been living by itself on the island for many years. Because it was very lonely, it added, it was relieved to finally gain a companion.

After getting to know the snake a bit more, the sailor asked if it had also been shipwrecked on that island. No, the snake answered. It was native to the island, which years before had been populated by hundreds of talking snakes like itself. There was plenty to eat, the weather was pleasant, and everyone was happy, the snake continued. But one day a flaming star suddenly fell on the island and exploded. All of the other serpents were killed, the snake sadly recalled.

For the next several months, the sailor and the snake shared the island and became close friends. Then, to their surprise, a ship anchored near the beach and some people came ashore, among them the sailor's two brothers, who had been searching for him. The sailor assumed the snake would jump at the chance of being rescued. But it refused, saying that it preferred to stay in the only home it had ever known.

The sailor was about to board the rescue ship when the snake said it wanted to give him a goodbye gift. It was a large treasure chest filled with jewels worth a vast fortune, which shocked the sailor. Hugely thankful, he bade his comrade farewell and returned to Egypt, where he enjoyed a marvelous life as one of the country's richest citizens.

Hearing this inspiring story significantly brightened the diplomat's mood. When shipwrecked on an uncharted island, the former sailor had at first feared that what was left of his life would be miserable. But in time, what had appeared to be misfortune turned out to be very fortunate indeed. The diplomat now applied this life lesson to his own situation. Maybe, he reasoned optimistically, the pharaoh would not be as upset with him as he had originally assumed. Thanking the man for telling his story, the diplomat prepared to face the king without fear.

The Most Famous Traveler

Although the tale of the sailor and the talking snake was broadly popular across ancient Egypt, by far the most often retold traveler's tale was "The Story of Sinuhe." The first known written version dates from around 1800 BCE, but it may have been passed along orally for a long time before that. The title character is initially seen as a minor officer in the Egyptian army, then commanded by the reigning pharaoh's son, Senusret.

SINUHE
The most famous traveler in Egyptian mythology, who runs away to a foreign land but eventually returns to Egypt

One night, the story goes, the army was camped in Libya (bordering Egypt in the west), and Sinuhe, who was out for a stroll, happened by Senusret's large, luxurious tent. There, the young man could not help but overhear the commander speaking with a royal messenger. The pharaoh had died, the messenger said, which meant that Senusret was now king. This news must be kept secret for the moment, Senusret warned the messenger.

Modern Adaptations of Sinuhe's Story

The ancient Egyptians were not the only ones who, in the fullness of time, have found the story of Sinuhe's adventures compelling. When the original texts of that tale were translated into European languages in the 1800s and early 1900s, a number of writers retold the tale in their own individual ways. Later in the twentieth century, several short stories and novels featuring Sinuhe appeared. One of those short stories, titled "Awdat Sinuhi" (meaning "The Return of Sinuhe"), was published in 1941 by Nobel Prize–winning Egyptian writer Naguib Mahfouz. Soon afterward, in 1945 Finnish writer Mika Waltari introduced a novel about Sinuhe's exploits titled *The Egyptian*. The work was so popular worldwide that in 1954 the Twentieth-Century Fox movie studio released a lavish film version, also titled *The Egyptian*. Even after more than seventy years, the film is still watchable, partly because, at great expense, the movie studio authentically reproduced the architecture, clothes, tools, weapons, and general atmosphere of ancient Egypt.

Sinuhe eventually missed his native Egypt and returned home. This picture shows him (at left) dressed in the clothing of the country where he had been living and drinking beer through a straw, as was the custom there.

The serious tone of Senusret's voice convinced Sinuhe that he might be severely punished, or perhaps even executed, if the new pharaoh found out he had overheard the conversation in the tent. In a panic, therefore, Sinuhe fled the camp. In the weeks that followed, he went back to Egypt and then headed northward into Retenu (now Syria).

In that foreign land, by pure chance, Sinuhe met and became friends with the local king, Ammunenshi. Partly because of that ruler's generosity, over the years the young Egyptian became highly prosperous. In one surviving ancient text, the myth

SENUSRET
The young pharaoh from whom Sinuhe flees

describes Sinuhe as an old man recalling earlier events of his life. He recalled that Ammunenshi "married me to his eldest daughter [and] made me chief of a tribe in the best part of his land [and] I passed many years, my children becoming strong men."[28]

When he reached his sixties, however, Sinuhe started to seriously miss his native land and asked the king to allow him to return there. Ammunenshi happily granted that wish, and Sinuhe traveled back to Egypt. At first he kept a low profile because Senusret still ruled that land. But soon the pharaoh found out that Sinuhe had returned. Much to Sinuhe's surprise, Senusret heartily welcomed him back. He should not have fled all those years ago, the ruler told him, as he would not have punished him for overhearing the secret. Pleased at this outcome, Sinuhe happily spent his last years in Egypt's capital, where he and the king he once feared became the best of friends. "I was in the favor of the king until [my last earthly day] came,"[29] the now famous traveler supposedly said on his deathbed.

Sinuhe's story was beloved by the Egyptians in part because it emphasized the importance of Egypt in nature's balance. The belief was that the gods had placed Egypt at the center of all things and the world's natural order. And when a native Egyptian moved to another land, he or she upset that natural balance. Moreover, in returning to Egypt such a traveler restored the divinely inspired order of things. In this way Sinuhe's tale, like so many other myths, reinforced an idea that all Egyptians held dear. As the late, great historian Lionel Casson put it, deep in their hearts they "regarded Egypt as the only place worth living in."[30]

SOURCE NOTES

Introduction: No Sense of History

1. Kerry Sullivan, "The Mythology of Nut, Mother of Gods," Ancient Origins, November 26, 2016. www.ancient-origins.net.
2. H.W.F. Saggs, *Babylonians*. University of California Press, 2000, p. 32.
3. George Hart, *Egyptian Myths*. British Museum, 1990, p. 7.

Chapter One: How the World and People Came to Be

4. Quoted in Hart, *Egyptian Myths*, p. 18.
5. James P. Allen, "The Celestial Realm," in David P. Silverman, ed. *Ancient Egypt*. Oxford University Press, 1997, p. 124.
6. Leonard H. Lesko, "Ancient Egyptian Cosmogonies and Cosmology," in Byron E. Shafer, ed., *Religion in Ancient Egypt*. Cornell University Press, 1991, p. 90.
7. Quoted in Josephine Mayer and Tom Prideaux, eds., *Never to Die: The Egyptians in Their Own Words*. Viking, 1938, pp. 24–25.
8. Quoted in Mayer and Prideaux, *Never to Die*, p. 25.
9. Hart, *Egyptian Myths*, p. 21.
10. Quoted in Miriam Lichtheim, ed., *Ancient Egyptian Literature: A Book of Readings*, vol. 3. University of California Press, 1980, p. 112.

Chapter Two: A Vast Array of Immortal Beings

11. Plutarch, *Isis and Osiris*, trans. Frank C. Babbitt, Bill Thayer's Website, September 7, 2020. https://penelope.uchicago.edu.
12. Judy Aitken, "Weighing the Heart," *Southwark Heritage Blog*, February 14, 2016. https://southwarkheritage.wordpress.com.
13. David P. Silverman, "Divinity and Deities in Ancient Egypt," in Byron E. Shafer, ed., *Religion in Ancient Egypt*. Cornell University Press, 1991, pp. 29–30.
14. Evan Meehan, "Egyptian Goddess Hathor," *Mythopedia*, November 29, 2022. https://mythopedia.com.
15. Or Graur, "The Milky Way Illuminated Ancient Egypt's Goddess of the Sky," *Scientific American*, April 8, 2024. www.scientificamerican.com.
16. Quoted in Nora E. Scott, "The Metternich Stela," *Metropolitan Museum of Art Bulletin*, April 1951, pp. 210–11.

Chapter Three: Death and Transfiguration on the Nile

17. Norma L. Goodrich, *Ancient Myths*. New American Library, 1960, p. 29.
18. Hart, *Egyptian Myths*, p. 33.
19. Plutarch, *Isis and Osiris*.
20. Rosalie David, *Handbook to Life in Ancient Egypt*. Oxford University Press, 2007, p. 142.

Chapter Four: Marauding Monsters and Mayhem

21. Quoted in Eric A. Powell, "The World of Egyptian Demons," *Archaeology*, May/June 2022. www.archaeology.org.
22. Quoted in Caroline Seawright, "Apep, Water Snake-Demon of Chaos, Enemy of Ra," Wayback Machine, April 4, 2004. https://web.archive.org.
23. Nitten Nair, "How Did Bastet Defeat Apep?," MythLok. https://mythlok.com.
24. Quoted in Joyce Tyldesley, *Daughters of Isis*, *Women of Ancient Egypt*. Penguin, 1995, p. 56.

Chapter Five: Famous Human Adventurers and Travelers

25. Quoted in Joshua J. Mark, "The Tales of Prince Setna," *World History Encyclopedia*, May 2, 2017. www.worldhistory.org.
26. Lewis Spence, *Ancient Egyptian Myths and Legends*. Dover, 1990, p. 190.
27. Mark, "The Tales of Prince Setna."
28. Quoted in Miriam Lichtheim, ed., *Ancient Egyptian Literature: A Book of Readings*, vol. 1. University of California Press, 1975, pp. 226–27.
29. Quoted in Lichtheim, *Ancient Egyptian Literature*, vol. 1, p. 233.
30. Lionel Casson, *Daily Life in Ancient Egypt*. American Heritage, 1975, p. 143.

FOR FURTHER RESEARCH

Books

Heather Alexander, *A Child's Introduction to Egyptology: The Mummies, Pyramids, Pharaohs, Gods, and Goddesses of Ancient Egypt*. Black Dog and Leventhal, 2021.

Marc Dresgui, *100 Amazing Facts About Egyptian Mythology*. Published by the author, 2024.

Future Publishing, *Ancient Egypt*. Future Publishing, 2025.

Jean Menzies, *Egyptian Myths*. Dorling Kindersley, 2022.

Louis Nelson, *Ancient Egypt*. North Star, 2025.

Lucas Russo, *Uncovering Egyptian Mythology*. Published by the author, 2022.

Philip Steele, *The Magnificent Book of Treasures: Ancient Egypt*. Weldon Owen, 2021.

Billy Wellman, *Egyptian Mythology for Kids*. Published by the author, 2023.

Internet Sources

Glencairn Museum, "Ancient Egyptian Creation Myths: From Watery Chaos to Cosmic Egg," July 13, 2021. www.glencairnmuseum.org.

K. Kris Hirst, "Osiris: Lord of the Underworld in Egyptian Mythology," ThoughtCo., September 4, 2019. www.thoughtco.com.

Joshua J. Mark, "Ancient Egyptian Religion," *World History Encyclopedia*, January 20, 2016. www.worldhistory.org.

Joshua J. Mark, "The Tales of Prince Setna," *World History Encyclopedia*, May 2, 2017. www.worldhistory.org.

Geraldine Pinch, "Ancient Egyptian Magic," BBC, February 17, 2011. www.bbc.co.uk.

Eric A. Powell, "The World of Egyptian Demons," *Archaeology*, May/June 2022. www.archaeology.org.

Rick Riordan, "Meet the Egyptian Gods," Rick Riordan personal website. http://rickriordan.com.

Jaden Song and Fares Mousa, "The Story of Anubis," Google Arts & Culture. https://artsandculture.google.com.

Bob Strauss, "Monsters and Mythical Creatures of Ancient Egypt," ThoughtCo., July 22, 2024. www.thoughtco.com.

Cierra Tolentino, "Egyptian Mythology: The Gods, Heroes, Culture, and Stories of Ancient Egypt," History Cooperative, December 30, 2024. https://historycooperative.org.

Websites

Ancient Civilizations: Ancient Egypt, National Geographic
https://education.nationalgeographic.org/resource/resource-library-ancient-egypt
This online presentation by the renowned National Geographic includes a collection of links to excellent articles on Egypt's ancient kings, gods, religion, pyramids, and much more.

Ancient Egypt Online
www.ancient-egypt-online.com
This very useful site features many links to separate articles about ancient Egypt, including ones on gods and their mythical stories, pyramids, mummies, temples, tombs, hieroglyphics, daily life, and more.

Ancient Egypt: The Mythology
www.egyptianmyths.net
Written and maintained by scholar April McDevitt, this site presents much diverse, accurate information about ancient Egyptian civilization. The author divides the site into five main sections: Gods, Myths, Symbols, Lands, and Resources each section contains multiple links to various subtopics.

Ultimate Guide to Egyptian Mythology, *Mythopedia*
https://mythopedia.com/guides/egyptian-mythology
One of the more reliable sources about ancient Egyptian myths on the internet, this one focuses on the Egyptian gods. Each article about a given deity describes their physical attributes, tells their principal myths, and discusses that god's impact on popular culture.

INDEX

PICTURE CREDITS

Cover: photoshooter2015/Shutterstock

4: Shutterstock.com
7: Science History Images/Alamy Stock Photo
11: Magica/Alamy Stock Photo
12: Bridgeman Images
17: Ivy Close Images/Alamy Stock Photos
21: Charles Walker Collection/Alamy Stock Photo
25: © NPL-DeA Picture Library/Bridgeman Images
27: Maryana Lyubenko/Alamy Stock Photo
30: The Stapleton Collection/Bridgeman Images
33: Lebrecht History/Bridgeman Images
35: Ivy Close Images/Alamy Stock Photo
39: Chronicle/Alamy Stock Photo
42: The History Collection/Alamy Stock Photo
44: Lebrecht History/Bridgeman Images
47: World History Archive/Alamy Stock Photo
49: John Frost Newspapers/Alamy Stock Photo
53: Peter van Evert/Alamy Stock Photo

ABOUT THE AUTHOR

Classical historian and award-winning author Don Nardo has written numerous acclaimed volumes about ancient civilizations and peoples. They include more than four dozen overviews of the mythologies of the Sumerians, Babylonians, Egyptians, Greeks, Romans, Persians, Celts, Aztecs, Norse, Chinese, Japanese, and others. Nardo, who also composes and arranges orchestral and chamber music, lives with his wife Christine in Massachusetts.